2025 copyright Loran Bateman-McKenzie

STOLEN
Before, During, and After

OPENING NOTE

You picked this up because something whispered:
This is about you.

Maybe you don't know what was stolen.
Maybe you do, but no one ever let you say it.
Maybe you never asked,
or maybe the question was too heavy to hold.

This book remembers.

For the names erased.
For the languages silenced.
For the joy that had to be hidden just to survive.
For the love that never learned how to bloom.

This is not history.
This is now.

Keep turning pages.
What was stolen...
is still speaking.

Table of Content

STOLEN 1

Before We Were Stolen 4

Stolen Voice 6

Stolen Name 7

Stolen Language 8

Stolen Self 9

Stolen Soul 10

Stolen Work 11

Stolen Invention 12

Stolen Wombs 14

Stolen Art 15

Stolen Childhood 17

Stolen Trust 19

Stolen from Africa 20

Stolen in Diaspora 21

Stolen by War 23

Stolen by War (Brother Turned Blade) 24

Stolen by War ("We Forgot We Were Family") 26

Stolen by Religion 27

Stolen from Indigenous Lands 29

Stolen in Camps and Ghettos 30

Stolen from Asia 31

Stolen from LGBTQ+ History 32

Stolen from the Poor 33

Stolen from the Disabled 35

Stolen Safety 37

Stolen Joy 38

Stolen Love 40

Stolen Memories (The Curse of Forgetting) 44

Stolen by Capitalism 48

Stolen by Capitalism 2 50

Stolen by Silence 52

Stolen by Shame 54

We Took It Back — Voice 56

We Took It Back 3— Name 60

We Took It Back 4 — Land 62

We Took It Back 5— Self 64

We Took It Back 6— Story 66

Still, We Rise 68

Still, We Create 70

Still, We Remember 72

The Great Human Theft 74

Before We Were Stolen

Before we were stolen,
we read and wrote in our own languages,

Before we were stolen,
we were productive members of our society,

Before we were stolen,
we built great nations and educated other nations,

Before we were stolen,
we were joyously exploring our universe,

Before we were stolen,
 we were members of loving families

Before we were stolen,
 we retold our history orally.

After we were stolen, we were stripped of our names and given numbers,
our tongues were beaten silent
until we dreamed in foreign syllables.

After we were stolen,
we tilled land we once would have owned,
bled into soil
and were told it was God's will.

After we were stolen,
our stories were buried under chains,
our gods renamed,
our heroes erased,
our maps redrawn without our footprints.

After we were stolen,
we became both weapon and wound —
taught to fear our own reflections,

taught to reach for freedom
like it was always a little too far.

After we were stolen,
we learned to dance with fire in our throats,
to birth resistance from song,
to braid survival into each other's hair.

After we were stolen,
we became myth and warning,
beauty and burden,
sorrow and defiance
carved into every generation.

Stolen Voice

Before we were stolen, our voices were law...
After we were stolen, we whispered to survive...
Now we speak louder than silence ever could.

Before we were stolen,
we spoke with thunder in our throats,
sang the seasons into rhythm,
called ancestors by name
and had them answer in wind.
Our words healed wounds, settled disputes,
welcomed birth, and buried the dead with honor.

Our voice was not loud —
it was sacred.
It built bridges.
It built us.

After we were stolen,
our mouths were taught to forget.
Tongues tied in foreign shapes,
punished for speaking home.
We were told our voices were too sharp,
too soft, too broken, too much.

So, we whispered in corners,
sang in secret, wrote poems in eyes
and protest in breath.

They said we were silent.
But we were **stolen** —not quiet.
And we are still speaking.
Even now.
Especially now.

Stolen Name

Before we were stolen, our names held worlds...
After we were stolen, they renamed us in ash...
Now we carry our truth in syllables we reclaimed.

Before we were stolen,
our names danced with the stars.
They meant *lion, river, first light, beloved*.
Our names carried the weight of lineage —
spoken with reverence, sung into birth, etched into stone and sky.
We were called into the world by those who loved us.

After we were stolen,
they branded us with names
not made for our mouths.
Cut our roots and stamped their own
into the soft soil of our becoming.

We were called *property, product, problem, thing*. Our names became numbers,
nicknames of mockery,
names we never chose.

And still—
we whispered our true names in sleep.
Taught them to our children
in rhythm and resistance.
Buried them in lullabies.

We are still remembering
how to name ourselves again —
not as survivors, but as the storm.

Stolen Language

Before we were stolen,
we painted the air with meaning.
Spoke in tongues sculpted by sun and soil,
words rooted in rhythm,
phrases layered like ceremony.

We had names for joy that took days to say.
Words for how the moon pulls at dreams.
Songs that held centuries
in a single refrain.

We translated the wind.
We negotiated with spirits.
We knew the weight of silence,
and when to let it speak.

After we were stolen,
our languages were outlawed, burned from books,
scraped from tongues, mocked as noise.
We were taught the conqueror's grammar
but not their mercy.
Taught their alphabet, but not their acceptance.
Our children cried in accents, we didn't recognize.
And we wept in syllables, we weren't allowed to teach.

But the language never died ,it went underground.
It lived in our drumming, in our food,
in the twist of our names, they couldn't pronounce.

Now, we are digging it up ,letter by buried letter.
We are writing again, not to be understood,
but to remember ourselves.

Stolen Self

Before we were stolen,
we were whole without explanation.
We knew who we were
before the world asked us to prove it.
We were spirit, tribe, lineage, role , woven into the land,
held by the names of our people,
defined by nothing but our being.

We belonged to something
that needed no permission.

After we were stolen,
they gave us masks and called them progress.
Told us to pick sides in wars we didn't start.
Taught us shame in our own skin
and pride in imitation.

They sold us back fragments of ourselves
in textbooks, products, and documentaries.
Labeled us exotic, savage, dangerous,
dependent on the lens.

They taught us to mistrust our reflection , to see distortion
where there was once only design.

But we are finding ourselves
in ancestral memories, in dreams that defy logic,
in art that doesn't ask permission.

We are rebuilding what was scattered,
and this time, we will name ourselves
before the world gets a chance to.

Stolen Soul

Before we were stolen,
our soul was not abstract.
It had shape ,woven from the laughter of elders,
the hum of harvest, the pulse of dance.

We did not question, whether we were whole.
We were born enough, raised in meaning,
wrapped in belonging.

Our soul was ceremony.
It was the fire in the center of the village,
the drumbeat at dawn, the quiet certainty of purpose.

After we were stolen,
they called our soul dangerous.
Called it primitive.
Called it wrong.

They caged it in doctrine,
broke it with fear,
shrank it down to guilt and obedience.

Told us we needed saving from ourselves.

But they never understood,
you cannot steal what you cannot name.
You can silence the song, but not the vibration.

Our soul stayed buried in breath, in movement,
in defiance that looked like stillness.

It waits for no permission.
And when we remember who we are,
the soul returns ,not as a guest, but as a reckoning.

Stolen Work

Before we were stolen,
we worked with the earth, not against it.
We knew the rhythm of sowing and resting,
the dignity of craft, the sacredness of sweat that fed our own.

We built not for wealth, but for community.
We labored with joy, and rested without guilt.

Work was prayer. Work was pride. Work belonged to us.

After we were stolen,
our labor became a commodity.
Our backs were broken for profit, our sleep rationed,
our time owned.

We picked cotton and were called lazy.
We built railroads and were told we didn't belong.
We cleaned homes we couldn't live in.
We raised children who would later forget our names.

We built their cities, their economies, their kingdoms
and disappeared from the credits.

But still,
we built for ourselves in secret , taught trades in basements,
cooked joy into meals, braided dreams into every unpaid hour.

We were never just labor.
We were architects, healers, engineers of survival.

And though they stole our time,
they could not steal the legacy
we worked into the bones
of every foundation.

Stolen Invention

Before we were stolen,
we imagined the stars before we could reach them.
We mapped rivers, measured time in shadows and flame, built
pyramids that whispered to the heavens, and roads that
remembered where we came from.

We cured sickness with roots.
We calculated seasons in stone.
We spoke to metal, to fire, to spirit
and turned them into tools.

After we were stolen,
they said we had no history,
no intellect, no science.

They took our blueprints
and signed their names in ink.
Took our medicine, and called it modern.
Took our designs, and sold them back to us
in plastic and patents.

They taught us their genius,
while burying our own.
Our inventors died unnamed,
our thinkers were made workers,
our dreamers imprisoned in silence.

But our invention never stopped.
It just changed shape.
It moved in code and cadence,
in rhythm and resistance,
in ideas passed like secrets
through generations that refused to forget.

Now we invent in full color,
with our names carved bold.
No more silence.
No more stolen light.

We are not only inventors.
We are the **origin**.

Stolen Wombs

Before we were stolen,
our wombs were sanctuaries.
They held lineage, not inventory.
They birthed names, not numbers.
Our mothers bled power,
and gave life surrounded by song,
by midwives who knew the stars,
by hands that caught legacy, with reverence. Children were not burden ,they were blessing.
Born into arms, that already knew how to love them.

After we were stolen,
our wombs were colonized.
Used, measured, bought.
Breeding grounds for empire, farms for future labor. Babies pulled from arms, before they were named.
Women forced to birth, for owners who called them asset.
Joy ripped into silence.
Milk taken from one child, to feed another
who would one day call her *nurse*, but never *mother.*

They did not just steal our bodies,
they tried to rewrite the beginning of our story.
But we survived.
And we kept birthing resistance.
In every cry, in every lullaby laced with memory,
we stitched freedom into generations, meant to forget.
Now our wombs are not silent.
They speak, they choose, they rise.

We are not just survivors of theft.
We are the beginning, and we remember.

Stolen Art

Before we were stolen,
we painted truth on skin and stone.
We danced grief into celebration,
sang memory into the air
so it would never forget us.
Our drums told stories before alphabets.
Our walls held color that outlived kings.

Art was not escape, it was *reality*.
Woven into worship, marriage, mourning,
harvest, healing.
It did not hang in museums.
It lived in us.

After we were stolen,
they called our art primitive,
then copied it in secret.
Took our sound, our rhythm, our movement,
and sold it, with our names removed.

We watched our dances on stages
where we were not welcome.
Heard our stories with new accents
and no footnotes.
Our patterns were fashion.
Our pain was aesthetic.
Our genius, a trend.

But we never stopped creating.
Even when they stole the spotlight,
we built our own stages.
Turned alleys into theatres, kitchens into studios,
grief into music.

Our art remembers.
It rebels, it reclaims, it revives.
And now, when we create, we sign it in full.
Unapologetic.
Unfiltered.
Un-stolen.

Stolen Childhood

Before we were stolen,
our futures were wide as sky.
We imagined in generations
planted trees we'd never sit beneath,
taught children to shape the world
not just survive it.

We dreamed without borders.
Named stars for our descendants.
Spoke in *when*, not *if*.
Our future was not a hope, it was a right.

After we were stolen,
the horizon shrank.
Our tomorrows became transactions.
We were told to be realistic.
To lower our eyes.
To reach for what we were allowed to have.

They gave us cages
and called them systems.
Set clocks ticking, on our potential.
Built schools that erased us,
then blamed us for not learning.

Our children were judged
before they could write their names.
Dreams became debts.
Visions became warnings.

But even so, we imagined anyway.
Built futures in poems, in protests, in pulses.

We dared to want joy.
We dared to teach our children to hope.
And hope, once taught, doesn't go quiet.

They stole our futures, but not our power
to make new ones.

Stolen Trust

Before we were stolen,
we walked kingdoms older than time.
Carved knowledge into bone,
spoke with the sky, built with stone and story.
We lived in harmony and hierarchy,
war and peace , but always *ourselves*.

We were black before the world made it a target.
We were not a color.
We were nations.

After we were stolen,
they unrooted us like weeds
and scattered us like ash.
Stacked us in ships like cargo, chained soul to body, and
renamed us *slave*.

They told the world we came from nothing,
even as we carried, iron will, sacred music,
ancient math, and gods too powerful to burn.

We were sold in lands we did not know,
forced to forget songs still humming in our blood.

But Africa was never lost , only buried.
It traveled in hips, in drumming,
in names we whispered into our children's hair.

We are the Diaspora, but we are not broken.
We are the map they tried to erase, and failed.

Stolen from Africa

Before we were stolen,
we walked kingdoms older than time.
Carved knowledge into bone, spoke with the sky, built with
stone and story.
We lived in harmony and hierarchy, war and peace
but always *ourselves*.

We were black before the world made it a target.
We were not a color.
We were nations.

After we were stolen,
they unrooted us like weeds, and scattered us like ash.
Stacked us in ships like cargo, chained soul to body,
and renamed us *slave*.

They told the world we came from nothing,
even as we carried, iron will, sacred music, ancient math,
and gods too powerful to burn.

We were sold in lands we did not know,
forced to forget songs still humming in our blood.

But Africa was never lost —
only buried.
It traveled in hips, in drumming,
in names we whispered into our children's hair.

We are the Diaspora,
but we are not broken.
We are the map they tried to erase
—and failed.

Stolen in Diaspora

Before we were stolen,
we were whole in place and name.
Belonging was not questioned, it was breathed.
We traced our ancestry in soil,
our worth in community,
our identity in memory that lived just down the road.

Home was not theory.
It was footsteps.
It was voice.

After we were stolen,
we were scattered like wind-born seeds,
blown across oceans
with no direction but survival.
We arrived with accents that didn't fit,
faces that stood out,
and names too hard for their tongues.

They asked,
"Where are you really from?"
Not knowing we were asking ourselves the same.

We became translators of pain,
bridges between two worlds,
never fully held by either.

We dreamed of a country, we only knew in fragments, longed for roots, in cities that kept moving.

But diaspora is not just dislocation,
it is reinvention.
We carry our ancestors in backpacks,
write history in new dialects,

raise children who speak in braided tongues
and still call us home.

We are the voice between generations,
the seed that learned to grow, with no soil
and still bloom.

Stolen by War

Before we were stolen,
we built lives that didn't need permission.
We drank tea slowly.
We grew vegetables in peace.
Our children played with wooden toys,
not shell casings. We argued over love, not borders.
We buried our dead when their time came,
not when someone dropped a bomb.

After we were stolen,
sirens replaced birdsong.
We slept with shoes on, bags packed.
We learned the names of weapons
before we learned the names of flowers.
Watched skies for missiles, instead of constellations.
War came in the name of freedom,
but took everything that made us free.
Our houses became rubble.
Our neighbors became memories.
Our memories became targets.

And still, we kept living.
We braided hope into bunkers.
We wrote poems in the margins of textbooks
we fled with.

They stole our peace, but not our humanity.
We still teach our children to plant seeds,
even if they might never see them grow.

Because peace is not the absence of war.
It is the decision, to remember what home feels like.

Stolen by War (Brother Turned Blade)

They didn't even have to invade.
They just handed us flags
and told us which side to bleed for.

Brother looked at brother
and saw enemy.
Not because we changed,
but because they gave us borders
and called it truth.

One family —
two nations.
Same language —
different loyalty.

They split the land
like it was a loaf of bread.
Told us which half we could die on.

And we did.

We built walls
that ran through graveyards.
We put up checkpoints
between bloodlines.

We started checking papers
on people who shared our mother's eyes.

We marched in uniforms
stitched from the same fear.
Pointed rifles at cousins
because someone else wrote the orders.

And they watched us —
from their balconies,

from their bunkers —
smiling.
Because they didn't have to kill us.
We did it for them.

We stole from ourselves
to prove we belonged
to someone else.

And now we're here —
scattered, scarred,
saluting ghosts.

This is what war really steals:
not land.
Not oil.
But the part of you
that used to believe
in *us*.

Stolen by War ("We Forgot We Were Family")

They told me *you* were the one to fear,
so I stopped seeing you as near.
They drew a line across our land,
put papers, guns, and rules in hand.

We grew up sharing jokes and bread —
now you're the name I shoot instead.
They gave us flags and uniforms,
then made our friendship feel like *warms*.

We speak the same, we laugh the same,
but now we play a deadly game.
I'm told to fight — but for what cause?
To guard some rule they made into laws?

They said, *"He's not your brother now."*
Just because of where he bows.
But deep inside I still remember
how we played ball in late December.

Now here we stand on different sides,
with wounds that don't fit in our pride.
I miss the days before this split,
before we let the world rewrite it.

We didn't lose to bombs or planes —
we lost when *love* got pushed through chains.
We lost when they made hate the rule,
and called our kindness weak or cruel.

But I still hope — and hope's not small.
That one day we break down the wall.
That one day peace becomes our sound.
That we find each other
on common ground.

Stolen by Religion

Before we were stolen,
we prayed with our feet in the river.
We spoke to the wind, to fire,
to ancestors who answered in thunder.

We didn't build cathedrals;
we walked through them.
Our altars were mountains.
Our temples were breath.

Our gods looked like us.
They came in many names.
And none needed fear to be followed.

After we were stolen,
they gave us one god, and many rules.
Said salvation had a language,
a skin tone, a tax.

Our ceremonies were called sin.
Our spirits called demons.
They baptized us in our own blood
and told us we were cleansed.

Faith became a leash.
A threat.
A bribe.

But still,
we found the divine in hiding.
In whispered chants.
In candles lit in secret.
In forgiveness we gave ourselves
when no priest would.

They stole our gods, and gave us shame.
But we are rewriting the scripture.
We are naming the holy,
in our mother tongues again.

Because belief, real belief,
was never meant to be forced.

Stolen from Indigenous Lands

Before we were stolen,
the land called us by name.
We walked with the seasons,
spoke to fire and river,
knew every mountain's breath,
every tree's spirit,
every silence between birdsong.

Our homes had no fences.
Our wealth was in stories, our wisdom in circles,
our treaties sealed with trust.
We were not lost.
We were **home.**

After we were stolen,
our homes became reservations, our gods outlawed,
our children taken and renamed.

They taught us their borders, and their shame. They built
monuments on bones, schools on scars,
cities on sacred ground, then asked why we didn't smile in
history books.

They called us primitive, as they dug gold from the mouths of
our mountains.
They drew maps, without asking the rivers
what they were called.

But we remember.
In language smuggled between generations,
in ceremonies held underground,
in land acknowledgments whispered
to the wind.
We are still here. We are the land.
And the land never forgets, her children.

Stolen in Camps and Ghettos

Before we were stolen,
we lived among our own , not perfect, but *possible*.
We walked streets where we were known,
shared meals that tasted like history,
spoke languages that held generations
in their vowels.

We buried our dead with ceremony.
We named our children with hope.

After we were stolen,
they herded us into corners of cities,
built fences of fear, called it order,
called it safety, called it *for our own good*.

They labeled us undesirable,
numbered us like livestock,
walled off our joy from the world
and then blamed us for the dust.

Camps. Ghettos. Zones. Quarters.
Every word a new way, to shrink a people. But even in tight
spaces, we stretched.
Made music with our breath.
Painted on broken bricks.
Taught math with twigs.
Braided resistance into lullabies
so our children would remember
they were more than where they were kept.

They tried to turn our neighborhoods into graves.
But we made them gardens.

Stolen from Asia

Before we were stolen,
we built empires on silk and ink,
calendars that mapped the heavens,
philosophies that shaped time.
We farmed rice in perfect rhythm,
traded across deserts and seas,
wrote poetry on bamboo
and wisdom into generations.

We honored elders.
We feared dishonor, not difference.
We knew who we were.

After we were stolen,
they came with flags and factories,
cut borders into our skin, took tea, gunpowder, languages
and called it discovery.

They made coolie of king, cheap of skilled,
and laborer of genius.
Brought us across oceans in ship bellies
not chained, but *bound* all the same.

In their lands, we were cooks, cleaners, quiet.
Too foreign to be welcome, too useful to be gone.
Mocked in cartoons, excluded by law,
jailed for building railroads, blamed for wars we didn't start.

But we learned their rules, then rewrote them.
Built temples beside laundromats.
Coded revolutions into math.
Held our accents like swords.
They tried to erase us, with caricatures and quotas.
But we drew ourselves again, in ink too bold
to be smudged.

Stolen from LGBTQ+ History

Before we were stolen,
we loved openly in the language of stars.
Danced in sacred circles,
wore both moon and sun.
Our stories lived in myth and memory
the twin-spirited, the shamans,
the warriors who loved other warriors.

We were not forbidden.
We were honored.
Our genders were fluid
like the rivers we bathed in.
Our love, a sacred rite, not a secret.

After we were stolen,
they called us unnatural.
Caged us in closets, burned us at stakes,
cured us with cruelty.
Wrote laws in stone and blood.

They erased us from textbooks,
cut our chapters from their history,
made us footnotes, or disease statistics.

But we persisted.
We loved in codes.
We held hands in alley shadows,
danced behind locked doors,
spoke in sighs that only the heart could hear.

They stole our history but, we wrote it back in drag shows,
in protest, in poetry, in chosen family. Now, we wear flags like
armor. We speak our names, without stuttering.

And we are not asking permission
to exist. We are **remembering**, that we always have.

Stolen from the Poor

Before we were stolen,
we had little, but we had *enough*.
We shared fish by the river,
bread at the doorstep,
laughter that didn't cost a thing.

We measured wealth in trust, in warmth,
in who would come when called.
We knew how to stretch a harvest.
How to make celebration from scraps.

After we were stolen,
our hunger became policy.
They called us lazy
while profiting from our grind.
Took our labor, but never our names.
Took our time, but never our futures.
They built wealth on our backs,
then blamed us for not climbing.
Made poverty a crime and charity a spectacle.
Divided us by color, accent, border,
but the wound was always the same:
a theft dressed as structure.

Still, we built anyway.
Shared anyway.
Raised each other's children
when systems would not.

We dreamed in full,
even when told to settle.
We made gold from grit,
beauty from broken.

They stole from the poor,
and called it progress.

But the poor remember.
And we are still here, with nothing to lose
but the chains we didn't choose.

Stolen from the Disabled

Stop speaking for me
like I didn't come with a voice.
Like I'm trapped in this body
so you get to choose, what I mean.

You look at me, and think:
pity, purpose, punishment, poetry.
But never *person.*

You narrate my existence
like I wasn't already writing it.

You say I'm "so brave"
for breathing.
You say "God has a plan"
because you're uncomfortable
with my body, and your privilege
sharing the same air.

Let's be honest, what you really fear
is that I have thoughts, you'll never understand.
That I know pain you'll never feel and still
I'm here.

Not broken.
Not waiting.
Just… *being.*

And still,
you talk over me
like I'm a radio
with no volume control.

You think slowness means weakness.
You think silence means nothing's there.

But inside this skin, there are empires of thought
you've never earned the right to witness.

My chair is not your symbol.
My cane is not your metaphor.
My diagnosis is not your lesson.

You stole my presence, with your assumptions.
You erased me in the name of help.
You held the mic, but never close to my face .

I'm not your project.
I'm not your sermon.
I'm not your feel-good social media caption.

I'm the part of the world
you still don't understand
because you never shut up long enough
to listen.

Stolen Safety

Before we were stolen,
we rested with both eyes closed.
Home meant haven.
Touch meant comfort.
The night held lullabies, not alarms.

Our bodies were not battlegrounds.
Our doorways did not need locks.
We walked freely, spoke freely, breathed freely.
Safety was not a request; it was our right.

After we were stolen,
we learned to check behind us.
To cross streets.
To carry keys like weapons.
To second-guess kindness.

We watched justice arrive late, or not at all.
Saw badges flash like threats.
Heard promises become prisons. We found danger, in
classrooms, in bedrooms,
in uniforms, in silence.

Safety became something we had to **earn**,
to fight for, to simulate. But our longing remains:
to sit in a room without armor.
To move through the world, without a plan to escape it.

They stole our safety,
but not our right to reclaim it.
And so we keep building sanctuary, even inside the ruins.

Stolen Joy

Before we were stolen,
our joy was unfiltered.
We danced for no reason but the beat.
Laughed loud enough to shake the sky.
We sang while working,
we celebrated the ordinary,
we found light even in the mud.

Joy was not luxury.
It was language.
It was culture.
It was *ours*.

After we were stolen,
they told us when to smile ,on command,
for their comfort, for their entertainment.

They took our music, and stripped it of meaning.
Took our fashion, and sold it back to us in glass windows.

They mocked our laughter, called us too loud,
too much, too happy for people who've suffered.

As if joy must be earned.
As if healing disqualifies pain.

But we still laughed.
We laughed in the fields.
In the margins.
At funerals.
In chains.
We laughed not because we forgot,
but because we **refused to be broken.**

They tried to steal our joy, but they didn't know
it grows back wild.
It shows up uninvited.
It dances barefoot, and it *never* asks for permission.

Stolen Love

Before we were stolen,
love was ceremony, not transaction.
We knew love in touch, in time,
in the way food was shared
before it was even tasted.

Love braided hair, gathered wood,
walked miles just to sit in silence.
It was abundant , not because we had everything,
but because we gave everything.

After we were stolen,
love was redefined for us.
It came with rules, papers, punishments.

We were told who we could love,
how to love, what love should look like
in someone else's mirror.

They taught us to hide love.
To fear it.
To silence it.
To survive without it.

We watched our families separated,
our affection criminalized,
our tenderness turned into weakness.

But still, we loved in secret.
In eyes across crowded rooms.
In hands held under tables.
In notes folded into coat pockets.

Love became rebellion.
It became *ours* again

in how we raised each other,
in how we chose family
when bloodlines were broken.

They stole our love, but they never understood
that real love doesn't obey.

It returns.
It multiplies.
It survives.

Stolen Memories

Before we were stolen,
we remembered through story.
We remembered in circle, in firelight,
in names repeated like prayers.

Our memory was communal
an echo passed down in food, in lullabies,
in the way someone tilted their head
just like their grandmother did.

We didn't need archives.
We were the archives.

After we were stolen,
they took our past, and replaced it with theirs.
Told us our story began with chains,
not with kingdoms.
Showed us their heroes, buried our own.

They banned our languages
so we couldn't remember.
Burned our books.
Beat the names of our elders
out of our mouths.

We became orphans
with living parents.
Strangers to our own ancestry.

And yet, our memories survived
in shadows and spices, in dances that made no sense
but still felt right.

We remembered without knowing how.
Dreamed of villages we never visited.

Felt homesick for places
we couldn't name.

They stole our memories, but memory is stubborn.
It returns in fragments, in feeling, in fire.
And we are learning to remember out loud again.

Stolen Memories (The Curse of Forgetting)

I don't know where I'm from.
Not really.

They told me my roots, are somewhere "over there" ,but never
gave me a map
that still made sense.

No names.
No tribes.
No village songs in my blood
just echoes that don't match the beat
of anything I've seen.

So, I pretend.
I pick flags like fashion.
Pick holidays like hashtags.
Say "my people"
like it means something,
when I don't even know
who my people were.

I wear dashikis
without knowing what the patterns say.
I scroll through history
like I'm begging for a breadcrumb
with my real name on it.

But it's not just lost, it was *stolen.*
Cut.
Erased.
Burned in classrooms, and rewritten in accents
that told me "You're just Black."
Just minority.
Just Other.

And somewhere in that lie
I learned to hate the mirror.
Learned to laugh at my own name.
Learned that forgetting, was safer than always remembering, that
I don't remember.

Because when you erase a people's past,
you don't just take their pride,
you steal their future.

If I don't know where I come from,
how do I know where I'm going?
How do I know what to honor,
or heal, or hold?

So, I carry this emptiness, like an inherited debt.
An ache passed down, by those who didn't forget
just couldn't say it out loud.

And now it's on me, to remember
what no one ever told me.

Stolen by Empire

Before we were stolen,
we governed ourselves —
not always perfectly,
but with memory, with balance.
We had our own systems,
our own justice,
our own gods.

Our maps didn't need straight lines.
Our borders breathed.
Our leaders led with stories, not swords.

After we were stolen,
they arrived with crosses and cannons.
Told us our faith was wrong, our laws savage,
our gold theirs.

They renamed rivers, redrew borders,
rewrote the very air.

Taught us to see ourselves, through their glass
blurred, broken, lesser.

We were colonized in body and mind.
Forced to kneel to a crown
we would never wear.
Made subjects on our own soil.

They taught us empire as enlightenment,
but it came wrapped in blood.
And silence.

But we remember.
Through the cracks of their concrete,
our roots still rise.

We speak our languages, even if only in dreams.
We paint our flags, even if only in spirit.

They stole by empire, but we reclaim by memory.
And memory, is undefeated.

Stolen by Capitalism

Before we were stolen,
we worked to live —
not to prove our worth.
We shared what we had.
Bartered.
Grew what we ate.
Rested when the sun said so.

Our value was not numbers.
It was presence.
Connection.
Enough.

After we were stolen,
time became a currency
we never had enough of.
We were taught to hustle,
to compete,
to wear exhaustion like a badge.

We sold our labor,
our culture,
our attention.
They branded our struggle
and sold it back to us
in commercials and slogans.

They told us success was possible —
if we just worked harder.
That poverty was a personal failing.
That dreams cost money
and rest was lazy.

We watched the rich sell hope
like a limited-edition product.
And we bought it
just to survive.

But now—
we are remembering.

That we are not machines.
That joy is not a luxury.
That community can't be monetized.
That wealth isn't just capital —
it's care.

They stole our time.
They stole our worth.

But we are reclaiming both.

Stolen by Capitalism 2

Before we were stolen,
value was shared, not hoarded or sold.
Time was a river,
not something controlled.
We built what we needed,
we gave what we had,
and no one went hungry
for dreaming too bad.

Now we are stolen,
every inch, every part —
our bodies, our habits,
our fears, our hearts.

They don't need chains —
just a click, a screen.
We're the product now
in this marketing machine.

Your scroll is a sale,
your selfie's a file,
your grief is a trend
if it stays up awhile.
Our pain is repackaged,
our joy is a pitch.
Your worth is your data —
your soul just a glitch.

The people are product.
The platform's the cage.
We dance for attention,
then sell off the stage.

We are the worker,
the brand, and the bait.
We're monetized motion
and five-second fate.

We are not free —
we are featured.
Not seen — just measured.
Not loved — just leveraged.

They steal us in daylight
with contracts and likes.
And we pay to perform
while they harvest the spikes.

But some of us see it.
Some of us feel
the cost of a heart
that they never let heal.

So, we log off.
We log in
to *each other instead.*
Build something they can't own
when the scroll goes dead.

Stolen by Silence

They never raised a hand,
they just **lowered their voice.**
Told us to calm down,
told us to *make a choice*
between survival and truth,
between dignity and peace,
between calling it out
or just letting it cease.

No bullets, no chains —
just *don't say a word.*
Erase the whole thing
like it never occurred.
Trauma? That's private.
Pain? That's yours.
Justice? Maybe —
but first do your chores.

They said,
"Don't bring that up, it makes people tense."
"Be the bigger person. Use your common sense."
"That was the past, why you still stuck?"
Because silence was **violence**
and we never got *unstuck.*

Our history's whisper,
our pain's on mute,
our culture's "cool,"
but our **truth's a dispute.**

And silence?
Silence is paid for in shame.
It's the handshake you give
while forgetting your name.

It's the secret you swallow
so *they* feel fine,
while it **kills you slowly**
line by line.

But no more.

We speak in caps.
We scream in rhyme.
We call it out, in real time.

We're done keeping quiet
so *they* stay okay.
Our silence was stolen —
and we ain't gonna **pay.**

Stolen by Shame

They didn't need to beat us —
they just taught us to hide.
To look in the mirror
and flinch inside.
To hush the pride,
to fear the skin,
to call what's natural
a **secret sin.**

They gave us rules
then broke our backs.
Told us we were "too Black,"
"too loud,"
"too fat,"
"too queer,"
"too wrong,"
"too weird to belong."
So we folded.
We edited.
We dimmed the song.

Shame is a cage with velvet bars —
you decorate it,
while it hides your scars.
You tell yourself you're fine,
you smile for the feed,
but inside?
You starve
and still call it **need.**

They stole our pride
before we even had a chance
to **wear it out loud.**

Made us pray to be smaller,
made silence feel proud.

Taught us guilt for surviving.
Taught us fear for desire.
Told us truth was selfish
and love was a liar.

But here's the thing:
Shame **doesn't survive** sunlight.
It shrinks.
It burns.
It **can't hold the mic.**

So we speak anyway.
We dance in what they tried to erase.
We show the scar
and the face.

They stole our light —
but we found the **fire.**

And shame?
Shame ain't louder than a choir
of people who finally
stop apologizing
for being **alive.**

We Took It Back — Voice

Before we were stolen,
we spoke like thunder under skin.
Our words were woven
into law, into lineage, into land.
We didn't raise our voice
because it was already **respected.**

Language was our inheritance —
spoken in proverbs,
carried in chant,
held in hush when sacred.

After we were stolen,
our voices were cut
from the root.
Tongues were punished.
Dialects demonized.
We were told our silence
was the price of peace.

We were misquoted,
talked over,
subtitled wrong.

We bit down on our brilliance
just to survive the room.

But now—
we took it back.

We took it back in poems
and protests,
in podcasts and pulpits,
in verses that refuse to ask permission.

We took it back
every time we sang in our mother's language
with the world watching.

We took it back
when we taught our children
that "loud" is not disrespect —
it's **survival.**

We took it back
by not lowering our tone
to fit the comfort
of the ones who muted us.

We are the echo they tried to bury —
and now we speak
in surround sound.

We Took It Back — Voice 2

They told us hush.
Told us blend.
Told us end the sentence
before we **begin.**

Said our words were too sharp,
too bold,
too much.
Too angry, too loud,
too hard to touch.

So we swallowed our syllables
and choked on regret.
Bit our tongues
until they bled a **debt.**

But guess what?

We spit that silence out.
Sharpened our sounds
into **shout.**
Tuned our throats like instruments,
turned pain into Parliament,
anger into elegance,
truth into **evidence.**

We took our voice back
from every stage we were denied.
From every job where we "didn't quite vibe."
From every table where we were the note
but not the **chord.**

Now we don't beg for the mic —
we build our own boards.

We speak like ancestors are listening.
We speak like daughters are watching.
We speak like the walls got ears
and *we* got rockets.

We ain't waiting on your invite.
We're not code-switching to survive.

We took our voice back —
and made it *amplified.*

We Took It Back 3— Name

Before we were stolen,
our names were rivers.
Given with vision,
blessed by elders,
wrapped in meaning
that sang for generations.

Our names meant *warrior, healer, sun after rain.*
They held the rhythm of our lineage,
the stories in our veins.

We were named with intention —
not convenience.

After we were stolen,
they stripped our syllables.
Stamped us with labels
that tasted like ash.
Called us *boy, girl, unit, slave,*
whatever made it easy
to forget we were made
of memory.

We were *renamed* to be erased.

Told to spell it different.
Say it "easier."
Laugh when they butchered it
just to make them feel bigger.

We memorized mispronunciations
like survival scripts.

But…

We took it back.

We started saying it louder.
Corrected the room
without apology.
Carved our full names
into every platform they said we didn't fit.

We tattooed them.
Chanted them.
Named our children in defiance,
in pride,
in **proof** that we remember.

We stopped shortening ourselves
to fit their mouths.

We reclaimed the song
they tried to skip.

Because this name?
This name is a map.
It is prayer.
It is protest.

And it is **mine.**

We Took It Back 4 — Land

Before we were stolen,
the land was not owned —
it was **known.**
Walked.
Named in wind and water.
Touched like a mother,
respected like a god.

We didn't draw borders —
we followed rivers.
We didn't fence it —
we listened.

The trees told time.
The mountains held memory.
And every path was a page
in the book of us.

After we were stolen,
they came with flags and farms,
measured soil in dollars and scars.
Called it discovery.
Called it manifest.
Claimed acres
like love could be surveyed.

They turned sacred into asset.
They paved over prayer.

We watched homes become holdings,
gardens become quotas,
forests become facts for extraction.

And still —
we whispered to the roots.

Now… we take it back.

Not always in title,
but in presence.
In seed.
In language that says
"this mountain had a name before yours."

We protest pipelines
and plant tomatoes.
We name our children after rivers
they tried to drain.

We return, not just to visit —
but to **revive.**

Because land is not real estate.
It is blood.
It is ancestor.
It is memory that breathes.

They tried to steal the land —
but forgot it already knew who we were.

And now…
so do we.

We Took It Back 5— Self

Before we were stolen,
we woke up without apology.
We knew our worth
before the world graded it.
We were not *becoming* —
we simply **were.**

Our bodies were temples
not trends.
Our minds were free,
unbent,
uncaged.

We walked with names that fit us,
skin we celebrated,
souls we didn't doubt.

After we were stolen,
they broke us into categories.
Told us who to be,
how to move,
what box to tick.

They taught us shame before language,
taught us to seek mirrors
that showed someone else's reflection.

They sold us a version of self
that only existed in their image.

But now…

We took it back.

Took back the mirror.
Took back the name.

Took back the softness
and the rage.

We stopped asking to be seen —
and started **being.**

We unlearned their story
and rewrote the script
with our scars as ink.

We became *whole*
not because they allowed it —
but because we refused to stay
in the pieces they left us in.

We are not what they stole.
We are what we **survived**.

And now,
we are **ours** again.

We Took It Back 6— Story

Before we were stolen,
we told our own stories.
We passed them in firelight,
in ceremony,
in songs where every note
remembered someone's name.

Our stories were maps.
Spiritual tech.
They weren't told to impress —
they were told to survive.

After we were stolen,
they rewrote our beginning.
Said we were savages,
said we were slaves first.
Cut out the chapters with kings,
healers, scholars,
mothers who moved nations
with a glance.

They filmed their version.
Taught it in schools.
Put it in books
and called it *fact.*

Told us,
"This is who you are now."

But they didn't know
we were still writing —
in margins, in memory,
in rhythm.

We took the story back.

Tore it from the textbook.
Wrote it in tattoos,
in music,
in mouths that once trembled
but now testify.

We made history bleed truth.
We made ancestry rise.

Our stories are not begging to be believed.
They're just **waiting to be heard**.

And now that we tell them again —
they're louder.
Bolder.
Whole.

Because we are the story.
And this time —
we hold the pen.

Still, We Rise

We were stolen —
voice, name, body, breath.
They rewrote us in chains,
taught us to fear our own reflection,
measured our pain
then sold it.

But still —
we rise.

We rose in fields we never chose.
We rose in classrooms not built for us.
We rose with backs bent,
souls cracked,
names misspelled
and futures redacted.

Still —
we rose

We rose in every generation that refused to forget.
In every ancestor who prayed for a moment
just like this.
We rose through dialect,
through diaspora,
through deserts of doubt
and oceans of erasure.

We are not luck.
We are not miracle.
We are not exception.

We are **the storm they said would never come back.**
And we walk on water now.

They tried to bury us —
but the seeds knew better.

We were stolen.
But still —
we bloom.

Still, We Create

They stole the canvas,
but we painted anyway.
On walls, on skin,
on whatever would hold the memory.

They stole the drum,
so we made rhythm with our bodies.
Clapped back against silence,
stomped grief into music
the world couldn't ignore.

They stole the stage,
so we danced in the street.
Sang truth through locked doors.
Wrote poems on the backs of eviction notices.

They said we had nothing.
But we made **everything**.
Culture. Style. Language. Light.
Turned scraps into scripture.
Turned broken into blueprint.

They burned our books —
but not the *story*.
They mocked our slang —
then **borrowed it**
with a price tag.

We are the rhythm in their radio.
The flavor in their food.
The twist in their fashion.
The gold in their algorithm.

We were never just labor.
We were always **genius**.

And we still are.

Because creation is our inheritance.
And no one can steal what keeps being reborn.

Still, We Remember

They erased the names,
but we remember.

They buried the bones,
but we remember.

They changed the maps,
renamed the rivers,
cut the tongues from our mouths —
but still
we remember.

We remember through recipes,
through rhythms,
through stories whispered
like prayers with no punctuation.

We remember when no one believed us.
When they called our history a myth.
When they made mockery of our pain
and turned our truth into trivia.

We remember in our hands —
in the way they braid, build, bless.

We remember faces we never met
but somehow *know*.
Languages we've never spoken
but somehow *feel*.

Memory isn't in books —
it's in breath.
It's in that ache in the chest
when you hear a song you've never heard
but somehow already mourn.

We are the memory
they tried to delete.
The download that wouldn't fail.
The drumbeat they couldn't mute.

They wanted us to forget
so they could move on.

But we **refused**.
And now?
We remember out loud.

The Great Human Theft

What if our greatness
is built on a graveyard?

What if every monument
was a mausoleum
with better branding?

We called it evolution —
but it walked like empire,
talked like conquest,
dressed like destiny.

We ripped from the womb of the earth
and called it civilization.
Tore stories from tongues
and called it education.
Chained brilliance to profit
and called it *progress.*

We taught machines to think
but forgot how to feel.

We mapped the stars
but forgot who we were
when we first looked up.

What if the only real genius
was in the hands we silenced?
What if the future we built
is just a high-tech shrine
to everything we buried?

We cloned wolves into pets.
Turned elders into algorithms.
We stitched flags over scars
and sang anthems

so loud
we drowned out the truth.

We became gods of industry
and infants of empathy.

We upgraded everything
except the soul.

And now we ask —
Are we the most intelligent species…
or just the most efficient thieves?

We stole art,
land,
labor,
names,
nations,
histories,
dreams,
even the idea of the divine.

We took and took
until taking felt like breathing.

And now we stand
on top of it all —
alone.
Impressive.
Imposing.
Empty.

If this is what it means to be "the greatest,"
then maybe
we misunderstood the assignment.

www.ingramcontent.com/pod-product-compliance
Lightning Source LLC
Chambersburg PA
CBHW040234110526
44582CB00002B/47